Kate Middleton
shows off a bikini
she wore while
vacationing in Ibiza
with Prince William
in 2006.

Kate Middleton

P<small>LATE</small> 1

Prince William
relaxes in "surfer"
swim trunks for the
couple's getaway to
Ibiza.

Prince William

PLATE 2

Kate wears a black-accented outfit to William's
graduation ceremony at Sandhurst in 2006.

PLATE 3

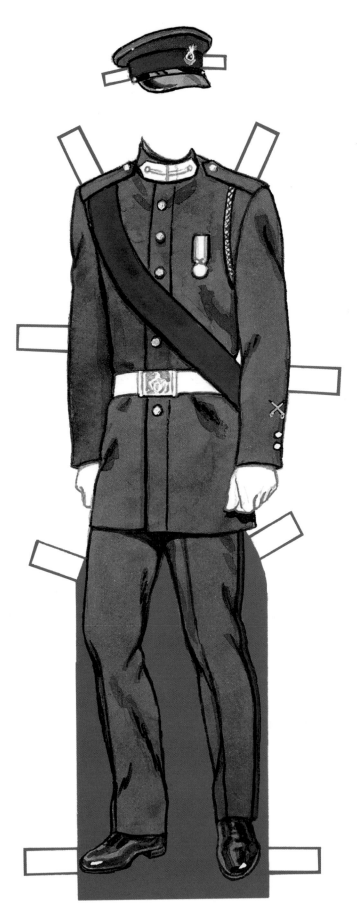

Prince William cuts a dashing figure for his graduation ("passing out")
from the Royal Military Academy, Sandhurst, in December 2006.

PLATE 4

A sparkling plunging-neckline dress that Kate acquired
during a 2007 Paris buying trip.

PLATE 5

A traditional outfit donned by William for the Annual Combined Cavalry
Old Comrades Association Parade (May 2007).

PLATE 6

Kate dresses in a glamorous gown for the couple's June 2008
attendance at the Boodles Boxing Ball charity event.

PLATE 7

Prince William wears his formal Household Cavalry Dress uniform
(he was commissioned in the Blues and Royals Regiment in 2006),
featuring his Royal Order of the Garter bandolier.

PLATE 8

Kate chooses this suit and cartwheel hat for William's investiture
as a knight in the Order of the Garter (2008).

PLATE 9

William's ceremonial robe and Tudor cap reflect his investiture as a
Royal Knight Companion of the Most Noble Order of the Garter.

PLATE 10

A double-breasted coat and boots were Kate's pick for the ceremony at which William received his wings in the R.A.F. in April 2008.

PLATE 11

William, dressed in his officer's uniform, was presented with his
R.A.F. wings by his father, Prince Charles, the Air Chief Marshal.

PLATE 12

Kate wears a pleated dress, jacket, and cartwheel hat to a friend's wedding that she and Prince William attended in October 2010.

PLATE 13

William's attire for a friend's wedding in October 2010 consists of a traditional morning suit with swallowtail coat, waistcoat, and pinstripe trousers.

PLATE 14

For their televised engagement announcement, Kate dons an "Issa"
dress, by Brazilian designer Daniella Issa Helayel
(all copies of the dress sold out in a single day).

PLATE 15

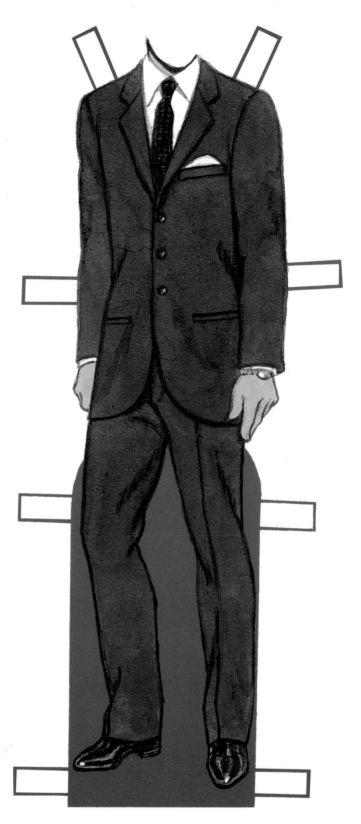

Prince William dresses in a single-breasted suit for the November 16, 2010, engagement announcement.

PLATE 16